Wonders of the Desert

Written by Louis Sabin
Illustrated by Pamela Baldwin Ford

This Book Belongs To

A Gift from the Kiwanis RIF Program

Troll Associates

Library of Congress Cataloging in Publication Data

Sabin, Louis.
    Wonders of the desert.

    Summary: Describes the animals and plants to be
found in the deserts of the world.
        1. Desert biology—Juvenile literature.
[1. Desert biology]   I. Ford, Pamela Baldwin.
II. Title.
QH88.S2   574.5'2652   81-7397
ISBN 0-89375-574-5   AACR2
ISBN 0-89375-575-3 (pbk.)

All day the sun beats down on the desert. The air above the sand and rocks is hot and shimmers. All is still.

Can any plants and animals live in this harsh, dry land? Surprisingly, many do.

Night is the time when the desert comes to life. At night, the starlit sky is clear. The heat of the day is gone. The air is very cool. Animals begin to stir. The first to appear are lizards and snakes, hunting for food.

The gecko lizard rests in the shade of a rock during the day. But after the sun sets, the gecko flicks out its sticky tongue to catch insects.

Another kind of desert lizard is the chuckwalla. When the chuckwalla is in danger, it squeezes into a narrow space between two rocks. Then, it gulps so much air that it swells like a balloon. It is stuck so tightly between the rocks that no animal can move it. The chuckwalla stays that way until danger is past.

The fringe-toed lizard protects itself in another way. The scaly edges on its toes make this lizard a speedy digger. If an enemy comes near, the fringe-toed lizard dives headfirst into the sand. It seems to swim out of sight in seconds.

Like lizards, most desert snakes spend the hot day in the shade. The sidewinder, a small rattlesnake that lives in the North American desert, comes out in the late afternoon.

The sidewinder got its name because it moves by whipping its body sideways. It's easy to tell where a sidewinder has passed—its body leaves marks in the sand.

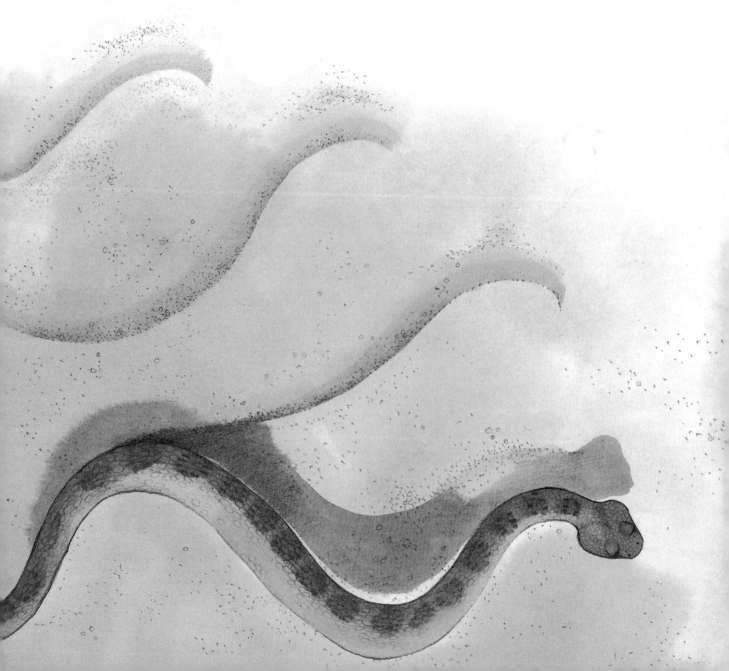

It does not rain very often in the desert. But when rain does fall, some animals appear as if by magic. One of them is the spadefoot toad. As soon as the weather becomes dry again, the spadefoot burrows backward into the sand. It makes a snug home under the ground and goes to sleep.

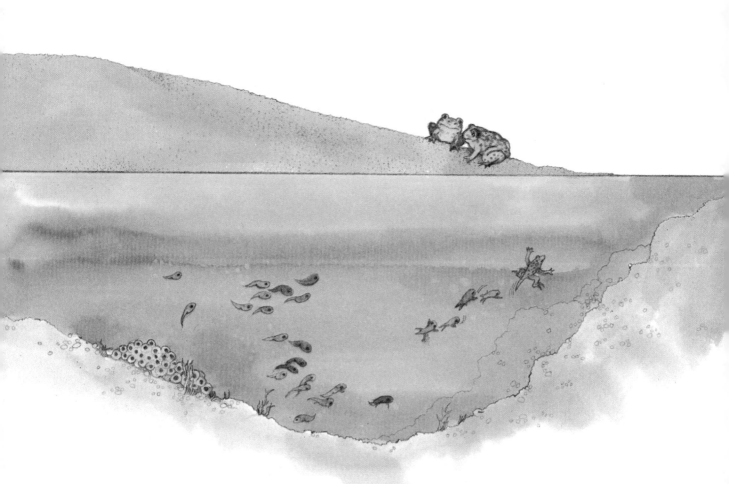

The spadefoot can sleep for almost a year. When there is a heavy spring rain, the spadefoot comes out and finds a newly made pond! The toad mates with another spadefoot, and the female lays eggs. In just one or two days, the eggs hatch into tadpoles. In less than four weeks, they are grown. By this time, the desert sun has dried up the pond, and the spadefoots must go underground.

Hundreds of different insects live in the desert. The black pinacate beetle—also called the "circus bug"—has a special way of dealing with enemies. It stands upside down and shoots out a bad-smelling odor!

The honey-pot ant lives on nectar from desert flowers. A few honey-pot ants eat this sweet liquid. Then they go back to their nest under the ground. They feed the nectar to other honey-pot ants. These other ants become living food tanks for the whole colony.

One of the most fearful creatures of the desert is the scorpion. It is usually two or three inches (5 or 7.5 centimeters) long and has a stinger at the tip of its tail. As soon as a scorpion has a victim in its claws, it raises its tail over its own back. Then it stabs its prey. Most scorpions are very poisonous.

Newborn scorpions climb onto their mother's back and are carried everywhere for almost a week. Then they are old enough to catch their own spiders, ants, butterflies, and grasshoppers.

One of the quickest desert animals is the roadrunner. This skinny bird, called the "clown of the desert," runs swiftly to catch all sorts of insects and lizards. The roadrunner can move at a speed of 20 miles, or 32 kilometers, an hour.

The roadrunner's foot has two toes that point to the front, and two toes that point to the back. This bird leaves a trail of X's. You can always tell where a roadrunner has been. But you cannot tell which way it has run.

The Gila woodpecker and the elf owl are birds that live in holes in cactus plants. The woodpecker pecks a hole in the cactus that is large enough for a nest. When the woodpecker moves to another cactus, the elf owl moves into the empty nest.

The tiny elf owl is a very smart hunter. It grabs the stalk of a plant and hangs upside down from it. Then the owl beats its wings to shake the stalk. This drives out all the insects resting there. Now the owl has plenty of food.

One of the biggest birds of the desert is the vulture. Flying high in the sky, the vulture has such fine eyesight that it can see for miles. When it spots a dead animal far below, it swoops down. By eating dead animals, vultures help to keep the desert clean.

The desert is home for many kinds of mice and rats. The kangaroo rat measures only 12 inches, or 30 centimeters, long, from the tip of its nose to the tip of its tail. It has short front legs and long back legs. It can jump more than 10 feet, or 3 meters, at a time. This tiny fellow also uses those strong back legs to kick sand at enemies. Kangaroo rats live mostly on seeds. They stuff the seeds into pouches in their cheeks, then take them back to their cool burrows under the ground.

The jack rabbit, like the rats and mice of the desert, does not drink much water. It gets all the water it needs from the plants it eats. When it is being chased, the jack rabbit can jump 15 feet, or 4.5 meters, in a single leap!

One of the jack rabbit's enemies is the coyote. It has a bushy tail and looks very much like a dog. At night, the coyote's lonely howl carries over the desert.

Desert skunks will eat just about anything—all kinds of fruits, insects, mice, birds, and dead snakes. Like its cousin who lives in the forest, the desert skunk protects itself by giving off a very smelly spray.

The desert is also the home of badgers, ground squirrels, wild pigs, foxes, and bobcats. And lots more. Almost all desert animals are small. That is because there is not enough food and water in the desert for big animals to live on.

All desert animals have special ways of surviving in the desert, and this is also true of desert plants.

The best-known desert plant is the cactus. Cactus plants have thick, shiny skin. They are covered with a kind of wax. The wax keeps the water inside the plant from drying in the hot sun. The thorns on a cactus protect it from hungry animals.

There are also many types of yucca plants in the desert. Some are small, and some are large, but most yuccas have long, spearlike leaves. The Joshua tree is the largest yucca. At least 25 kinds of birds build nests in the Joshua tree.

Spring rains bring color to the desert. White daisies, pink primroses, and purple verbenas spring to life. But this beauty does not last long in the heat of the summer sun.

Most desert trees send roots deep into the ground to find water. The roots of the mesquite tree can grow as far down as 100 feet, or 30 meters.

In the deserts of North Africa there are many palm trees. People eat the dates that grow on these trees; then they grind the date pits to make a drink. Palm leaves are used to make baskets, and the stems to make rope. When a palm tree dies, the wood is used to build things and to make fires. Every part of the tree is used.

Palm trees need a lot of water to stay alive. That is why they grow only where water is not too far down in the sand. A place in the desert where palm trees grow is called an oasis.

People called nomads often wander from oasis to oasis. In fact, *nomad* means "wanderer." Some nomads are shepherds. Others are traders, carrying things to sell.

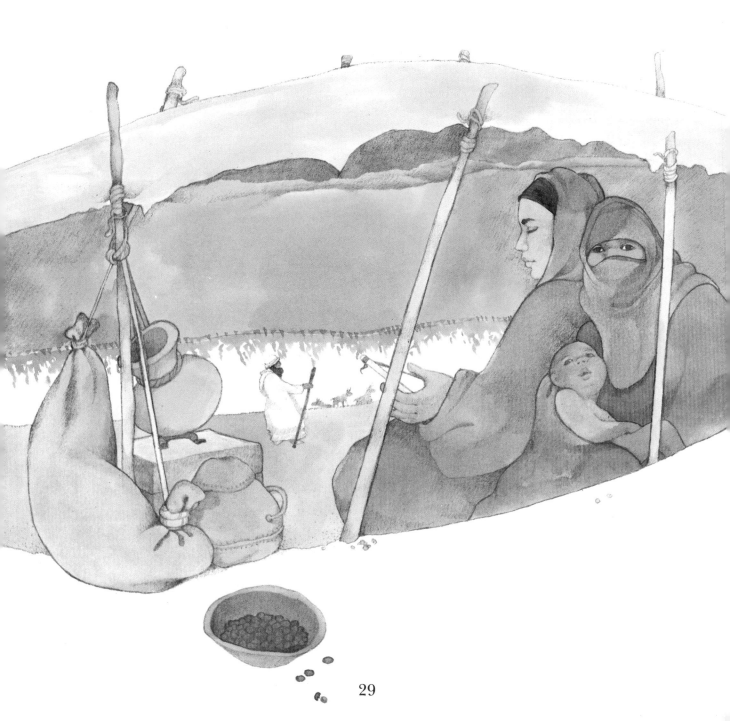

The nomads face very harsh conditions in North Africa's Sahara Desert, where sand dunes are hundreds of feet high and miles long. When a strong wind blows, the sand of the dunes fills the air. It is impossible for a person to see in a sandstorm. Travelers must stop and wait for the storm to end. The nomads are not as well-suited to the desert as the animal they ride—the camel.

The camel is the perfect desert animal. It moves easily over the sand on wide feet. It has long lashes to keep sand out of its eyes. And it can shut its nostrils to keep sand out of its nose.

At an oasis, a camel can drink 25 gallons, or 95 liters, of water in only a few minutes! Then it is ready to go without water and food for many days. It does this by living off the fat in the hump on its back.

The desert is a hard place to live in for people, animals, and plants. Yet there is beauty as the sun sets purple and red over the windswept sand. There is beauty in the colors of snakes and lizards and cactus flowers. And there is beauty in the flight of the hawk that soars far above the desert. It all makes the desert a very special home.